The Virginia Water Picture Book

by

Ron and Dorothy Davis

Dedicated to the people of Virginia Water past and present

Published by Egham-by-Runnymede Historical Society

ISBN 0-9508234-4-9
Printed by Ian Allan Printing Ltd, Coombelands House,
Coombelands Lane, Addlestone, Surrey

INTRODUCTION

The parish of Virginia Water, carved out of the parish of Egham in 1838, consists of the old estates of Portnall and Wentworth, now the Wentworth Golf Club and Estate, the hamlets of Stroude, Trumps Green, Knowle Hill, Callow Hill and Shrubbs Hill and a small piece of Windsor Great Park. We have in addition ventured a short way further down the A30 to include the area known as Broomhall, for it plays an important part in Virginia Water's history and was itself part of the old parish of Egham. The photographs come from various sources: about a third are from The Egham Museum's collection, but the book would have been poor indeed without the items from private collections and family albums. We are extremely grateful to the collectors and families who allowed us access to these obviously treasured pictures. Of particular interest are the photographs attributed to William End who opened his photographic studio in Whitmore Lane, Sunningdale, in 1895 and started a family business that lasted for 90 years. We are indebted to John End for permission to use these.

Ron and Dorothy Davis
September 1989

ACKNOWLEDGEMENTS

The authors' thanks are due to all those people in Virginia Water, Stroude, Sunningdale, Egham and elswhere who so generously shared their memories, their research or lent or donated photographs: Mr Armstrong, Vivian Bairstow, David Barker, Keith Barkham, the late Len Barkham, Lesley Barkham, Elaine Barrington-Hudson, Stuart Bennett, Alfred Bishop, the late John Blades, Jane Burn, H. C. Casserley, Chertsey Museum, Marie Chitty, Reg Cox, Graham Dennis, Jane De Salis, the late Jerome De Salis, Harold Dorman, Richard Doyle-Davidson, Phyllis Edge, The Egham Museum Trust, John End, Leslie and Dorcas Goodwin, Kay Green, Cyril Greenslade, John Hammond, John Hardaker, Tim Hayes, W. J. Highgate, Donald Ing, Jean Jarvis, Kathleen Kennerell, Mary Lee, A. E. Leigh, Ron Littlefield, Adrienne Lumb, M. Pamela Mikhelson, Amy Mitchell, Jennifer Mitchell, The S. A. Oliver Charitable Settlement, Bernard Pardoe, Louisa Parker, the late S. F. Plumb, Norah Prior, Stuart Ralph, Beth Spencer, Mavis Swenarton, Arthur Teasell, Win Trowbridge, Robert Walker, Mercy Watkins, Joy Whitfield, Jill and Richard Williams, Hugh Wyatt and the staff of Barton & Wyatt, Virginia Water and any others inadvertently omitted: to the Press Association Ltd for the picture at the top of page 32: to the Royal Commission on the Historical Monuments of England for the lower picture on page 44: to British Greeting Cards Corporation Ltd for the lower picture on page 28: to Sport & General Press Agency for both pictures on page 33: to Surrey Herald Newspapers Ltd for the lower picture on page 55: to Times Newspapers Ltd for the picture at the top of page 60: to Joan Hooper for manuscript typing: to Joan Bairstow for lettering. Where any possibility of copyright ownership exits, attempts have been made to contact the owner(s). Apologies are due if any do exist of which the publishers are not aware.

Egham-by-Runnymede Historical Society is a registered charity No 257294.
Net proceeds from the sale of this book will go to further its charitable purposes.

OTHER PUBLICATIONS BY EGHAM-BY-RUNNYMEDE HISTORICAL SOCIETY
Country School by Dorothy Davis
A Correct List of all the Coaches Passing through Egham 1828
Egham Races by Maurice E. Lord
The Egham Picture Book by Dorothy Davis

The 21-mile stone in the parapet of Cascade Bridge on the A30 opposite Virginia Water.

VIRGINIA WATER *the woods 1920*

John Speed's 1610 map of Surrey shows only three names in the present parish of Virginia Water: Portnall, Trotsworth and Stroude. The same names appear in the early registers of Egham Parish Church to identify the inhabitants of this, the western corner of the old parish. One must assume that Portnall, meaning 'Podda's nook', the western part of Wentworth golf course, Trotsworth, meaning 'Trot's enclosure', in the vicinity of the present railway station, and Stroude, meaning 'the marshy land overgrown with brushwood', were to our Saxon forbears the most fertile enclaves in an otherwise unproductive environment, where brambles, bracken and silver birches grew more readily than wheat.

BROOMHALL LANE *Sunningdale c.1905*

This delightful rural scene with Noakes' Corner on the left, a thatched cottage demolished in the early years of this century, is the extreme western edge of the old parish of Egham. Somewhere in this vicinity a small nunnery was established in the 13th century in the area known as the 'menechêne rude' or 'nun's clearing'. The nuns, often called the 'nuns of the forest', supported their house by leasing out their lands, including the Portnall estate in Virginia Water, to tenant farmers. Being on the main road to the west they would have provided succour and shelter to travellers. Theirs was clearly a daughter house to Chertsey Abbey for, sometimes unwillingly, the monks provided them with ale and bread weekly. Broomhall Nunnery was always a poor house and was dissolved in 1522, before the great dissolution of the monasteries, its prioress, Joan Rawlings, receiving a pension of £5 per annum. Most of its lands were used to endow and maintain the new college of St John at Cambridge, but two Egham gentlemen had already cheated the nuns out of Portnall.

WARREN FARM *East Drive 1922*

This is probably Virginia Water's oldest extant building and may date back to the early 17th century. On the earliest Ordnance Survey maps it is called Clayford Farm, a rather odd name not occurring in any other known sources. Perhaps Clearford Farm was intended, Clearford being where the Bourne crosses Wellington Avenue. Earlier the property had been known as Lower Portnall Farm. When the Countess de Morella of Wentworth purchased the property in 1891 the name was changed to Warren Farm. There were at least two warrens on what is now the Wentworth Estate and in the 18th century Henry Cole of Portnall Park made his living by breeding rabbits commercially. Robert White of Chobham came before Richard Wyatt, the Chertsey magistrate in 1776, accused of stealing one of Mr Cole's rabbits from a hutch trap.

WARREN FARM *1920s*

Before 1891 Lower Portnall Farm was the home of the estate carters. After the countess purchased the premises in 1891 and the name was changed it remained in use as the base for the carts and the working horses. Frank Curtis and his wife continued this tradition for many years in the first half of the 20th century. Just after the First World War, Mrs Curtis, seen here with one of her horses, appeared in a pageant procession as Britannia, using a horse and cart from the farm as her chariot. The procession was organised by John Chapman of Warren Lodge and started from a field in Lyne Road, ending up in the present King George VI Playing Field. Tea was served from Cabrera Cottages. The association with horses continued into the 1950s and 1960s when Captain Richard Ambler ran a riding school from Warren Farm.

WARREN FARM OUTBUILDINGS *1920s*

Here John Blades, Frank Curtis's grandson, is seen feeding chickens. The large barn in the background fronted on to the footpath to Knowle Hill but has since been demolished.

WARREN FARM *1980s*

Mrs Maud Cox, Frank Curtis's daughter, and her husband lived at Warren Farm into the 1960s. Although water had been laid on, replacing the well and pump, they had no electricity and used oil lamps for lighting. After they moved out the house was boarded up and for some time remained derelict. A lady came to the rescue. While house hunting in the district Estelle Matthews saw it, realised its potential and persuaded her husband, Charles, to have it restored. It was virtually taken apart and put together again. A few alterations were made, two dormer windows being added into the line of the roof.

OLD BUILDING

possibly old Trotsworth farmhouse c.1892

The shape of this 'deserted house near Virginia Water station' accords with the ground plan of Trotsworth farmhouse on the Poor Law map of 1856. The building would have been one of a long line of farmhouses, stretching back to the possible site of the old manor house of Trotsworth. Trotsworth was the only Virginia Water manor, a sub-division of the Manor of Egham. It was a poor manor, having only to provide a quarter of a knight in time of need and therefore paid in cash. In the 12th century this would have been 5s. The lord of the manor, as is usual, retained mineral and hunting rights while a succession of tenant farmers pursued a mixed agricultural economy on the hungry soil.

CHRISTCHURCH ROAD *1920*

Christchurch Road, once the Thorpe and Chertsey Road, went through the middle of the Manor of Trotsworth. The northern boundary of the manor was Hollow Lane, the eastern, roughly the line of Trumps Green Road and the western, Callow Hill and Wellington Avenue. On either side of this road stretched the Trotsworth Farm fields; now it is flanked by houses, a development started by W. G. Tarrant in the 1920s. The field, seen here under cultivation, was referred to as Ten Acres. At the junction with Callow Hill on the right of the picture a stretch of woodland was called Packers Grove. This name was adopted by Dr Michael Loxton when naming his new surgery in Christchurch Road. A nearer field on the right was called Kiln Copse, no doubt owing its name to its proximity to the Trotsworth brickworks in Hollow Lane.

TROTSWORTH FARM OUTBUILDINGS *1920*

Thomas Whitfield, whose lease on Trotsworth expired in 1865, sold up all his farm stock: poultry, 200 sheep and lambs, 24 pigs, only five milking cows and his eight 'good working horses'. The list of farm implements shows that he planted both wheat and root crops and made butter, cream and beer. Farmer Whitfield also sold his 'superior double-barrelled gun by Manton, with mahogany case and fittings'. When the farm became the headquarters for the builder, W. G. Tarrant, the outbuildings were used to store building materials. During the Second World War food supplies were kept there.

TROTSWORTH FARMHOUSE *1920*

In September 1861 the Count de Morella of Wentworth bought the Manor of Trotsworth. He appointed Andrew Blake from Scotland as land steward. All the count's assets passed on his death in 1877 to his countess and she had the house in the photograph built in about 1885. Like the rest of the Wentworth estate it was inherited by the countess's youngest child, Ada Constance Beatrice, who claimed to be Lady of the Manor of Trotsworth. During her partnership with W. G. Tarrant, the Byfleet builder, that resulted in the development of modern Wentworth, this house was the works office. It was pulled down at the end of the 1950s and the modern block of flats, Trotsworth Court, built on the site.

TRUMPS MILL *Trumps Mill Lane c.1969*

From medieval times there was a mill called Trumps on the Bourne stream. Its land was partly in the old Egham parish and partly in Thorpe. In 1617 when the manor was surveyed for a new tenant the mill was valued at £17. When the new church at Virginia Water was almost finished in 1838 the then owners of Trumps Mill, Corpus Christi College, Oxford, wrote to ask if the mill would be included within the new parish boundary. If so they wished to become subscribers. The mill itself is just in Thorpe parish, but as the new church would be nearer than St Mary's, Thorpe, the labourers in the vicinity of the mill were welcome to join the Virginia Water congregation. Another mill operated at the point where the River Bourne crossed the Great Western Road. It was known as Harpesford meaning 'the ford on the main or war road'. In medieval times there was a bridge over the river which the Abbot of Chertsey was expected to keep in good repair for travellers. When George III decided to repair and enlarge the lake in the 1780s Harpesford Mill and neighbouring cottages were bought by the Crown and 'overflowed' in the creation of the new Virginia Water. At the same time as Harpesford was flooded the boundary of Windsor Great Park was extended and the Great Western Road diverted a few hundred yards.

Photographer: Vivian Bairstow

THE GREAT WESTERN ROAD
Sunningdale looking west c.1910

The photographer stood on the very boundary of the old Egham parish as the small coach moved off westwards. The road, as the gateway to the south-west, was a source of great prosperity to those who lived on it. Under the Highway Act of 1728 the Bedfont and Bagshot Turnpike Trust had control of the road from Hounslow to Bagshot. Local gravel pits were used as a source of material for road maintenance. After 1875 responsibility for repairs to the road reverted to the parish of Egham. A large number of stage-coaches passed along the road bringing trade to the inns until 1856 when the railway came, virtually extinguishing the need for stage coaches. The horse became the motive power for journeys to the new stations. Sunningdale station can be seen in the distance. The photograph also illustrates the rapid development of another means of communication — the telephone. At this time all lines were overhead, the poles in the picture carrying as many as 128 lines for communication to Basingstoke and beyond. On the right of the picture is Noakes' Corner and on the left the garage, run by Edward Halfpenny. The boundary between Surrey and Berkshire at this point runs more or less to the north of the Great Western Road apart from a small circular indentation extending from Surrey into Berkshire down Broomhall Lane.

Photographer: P. O. Collier

THE CHEQUERS INN

Sunningdale looking east c.1905

Inns were required along the road where travellers might rest, take refreshment and change their horses. The journey, however, could be perilous. On 17 January 1774 a Dorset linen-draper rode on his mare towards London on business. It becoming dusk he stopped off at the Chequers, then known as the Bromwell or Broomhall Hutt, a property of more than an acre including outbuildings and stabling. According to the licensee and his staff the gentleman stayed about half an hour, then with the help of the ostler, he buckled his saddlebags on again and set off towards Egham in the gathering darkness. He was never seen again. By the time Alfred Halfpenny took over at the end of 1901, travelling was less dangerous and more civilised. Halfpenny was a true turn-of-the-century man. He offered good stabling at the inn to horse-drawn travellers as well as the ancient crafts of coach-builder, farrier and blacksmith, yet at the same time he looked ahead to the era of the motor car. Within a few years the motor garage advertised last on his placard was to take over the corner site. The board on the left denotes that St John's College was disposing of some of the extensive Broomhall lands it had acquired in the 16th century but was retaining a leasehold to bring some income.

Photographer: P. O. Collier

THE RED LION *Shrubbs Hill c.1905*

Shrubbs Hill is one of our oldest place names, like Podenhale and Harpesford, being listed in a medieval version of the bounds of old Egham parish as granted to Chertsey Abbey. This photograph shows the old Red Lion, the next hostelry from Broomhall on the way to London. In January 1775 two Chertsey men pursued a highwayman, who had allegedly robbed one of them, to the Red Lion and apprehended him there. Other witnesses came forward to identify him as the man who had robbed ladies driving in common post chaises. His horse, left in the Red Lion stables, was also recognised. Although denying the charges, the highwayman was convicted at Kingston Assizes three months later and sentenced to death.

Photographer: William End

THE WHEATSHEAF INN *London Road c.1900*

In 1768 the first Virginia Water, constructed by William, Duke of Cumberland after his victory at the Battle of Culloden in 1746, burst its dam and flooded the neighbourhood. In the ensuing confusion one John Atkins built an inn, called the Wheatsheaf, on the edge of Windsor Great Park advantageously sited near the main road. Some years later with a new lake designed, the Crown was desirous of buying Atkins out and extending the park pales beyond his property. He, however, a natural business man, kept increasing the price. In addition the Wheatsheaf became the unofficial headquarters for William Tough, the Foreman of the Works, while he was directing the digging and landscaping of the new lake. Whatever the reason the inn survived. In June 1801 George III, Queen Charlotte, Prince Adolphus and an unnamed princess visited the Wheatsheaf. The ladies remained at the inn, while the King and his son were taken to see the progress of the work at 'the Pond Head'. According to Mr Tough, His Majesty thought the water remarkably pleasant. In the photograph the hotel staff are seen greeting the arrival of a coach, a nostalgic reminder of the past.

THE WHEATSHEAF INN *London Road c.1910*

Culling Charles Smith of Wentworth's became the new owner of the Wheatsheaf. Following the Egham Inclosure Act of 1814 he acquired about a quarter of an acre of land adjoining the inn and a year later mortgaged the whole property to a Windsor brewer for £1,500. In 1826 he sold the inn and the land to the Crown for £5,000, out of which he had to pay off the mortgage. The Windsor brewers, Ramsbottom & Legh, remained the tenants. By the 1840s, when Louisa Baker was the landlady, the brewers, Neville Reid & Co, had taken over. There was trouble in 1851 when it was found that the innkeeper was charging the public for going through the gate into Windsor Park and employing two disreputable characters as guides. A go-ahead individual called Henry Jennings was landlord in 1852 and anxious to keep a good house. He indicated that he would like to take over the lease from the brewers. With the coming of the railway in 1856 he anticipated more trade from a superior type of person but all Neville Reid was prepared to spend was £250. In 1860 Jennings got his lease for 42 years. Two years or so later the property was enlarged. However, there was no water for flushing the water closets and so a hydraulic ram was installed near the bottom of the cascade to raise water to the inn. The inn appears to have flourished until the First World War when licensing restrictions and a general shortage of customers forced the landlord, Robert Upcraft, to ask for a rent reduction. After the war his daughter, Louisa, took over and was soon making plans for a petrol station across the road.

AERIAL VIEW OF THE WHEATSHEAF *c.1933*

On the lower right hand side of the picture are the stables of the Wheatsheaf hotel. The area of land, on which the Amoco service station now stands, was rented from the Crown Estates by the proprietor of the Wheatsheaf hotel as a drying ground for laundry. In the 1860s the size of the plot (originally two acres) was increased to accommodate more kitchen garden. This included a small piece of land behind a toll house. After 1865 additional stables were built on this side of the road together with pigsties. The buildings, which enclosed a cobbled yard, were demolished when the service station was extended in the 1970s.
The growing popularity of the motor-car after the First World War demanded better road surfaces and the macadam ribbon of the A30 gleams. More visitors came to the lake and in 1928 a tea-house was opened opposite the Wheatsheaf on land owned by W. G. Tarrant Ltd. It was immediately popular with tourists and locals alike and by 1935 had extended its facilities to include a restaurant, petrol station and a swimming pool. Its cheerful 'Hollywood Spanish' appearance, like the High Street Odeons, typified an age of defiant leisure as Europe faced the threat of another war. In 1939 the tea-house was occupied by Gavin Fairfax Ltd who added a motor showroom to its amenities. During the Second World War it became a small factory. After the war it experienced varying fortunes: was run as a casino, was seriously damaged by fire and finally rebuilt and opened as a restaurant.

STAFF AT THE WHEATSHEAF *1898*

When this picture was taken the Wheatsheaf inn was at the height of its prosperity. In the centre is the manageress of the establishment and on her left the cook. On her right is Harriet Adelaide Burr who had come down from London to work as the inn's book-keeper/barmaid. To save her walking the two miles or so from the station alone or having the expense of hiring a gig, young Robert Trowbridge then living at Pinewood Lodge, offered to accompany her. They eventually married and remained in the area all their lives.

FORT BELVEDERE *Shrubbs Hill c.1930*

As part of the design for the first lake a belvedere was built in about 1750 on the south eastern boundary of Windsor Great Park at Shrubbs Hill. As its name suggests, it was a viewpoint from which to admire the picturesque scenery of the lake. In the reign of George IV it was enlarged and converted into a mimic fort. An imposing array of cannon was set up on a platform around the tower. The guns were cast at Woolwich between 1729-49 by Andrew Schalch. The cannon fired salutes on royal occasions, often answered by the guns of the model frigate on the lake.

ROBERT TURNER *Master Gunner 1900*

During the 19th and early 20th centuries the bombardiers charged with firing the ceremonial salutes were service pensioners. They earned 2s 6d a day, the same wage as a labourer, for carrying out these peaceful military duties. They lived in a cottage, at that time attached to the fort. In the 1850s and 60s James Tait from Scotland was in charge. He was a Chelsea pensioner and had served as a sergeant in the Royal Artillery. He was succeeded by Robert Turner, also a pensioner, who is seen here, in ceremonial dress, firing the guns in honour of Queen Victoria's 81st birthday. F. C. Hodder reported in *A Short History of Sunningdale* that Mr Turner was a Crimean War veteran and that he and Mr Tait together had been in charge of Fort Belvedere for a total of 84 years.

Photographer: William End

FORT BELVEDERE *c.1966*

In the 1930s Edward, Prince of Wales, later King Edward VIII and later still Duke of Windsor, made the Fort his permanent home. Extensive alterations were made, retaining the outward appearance but transforming the inside to the highest standards of comfort and elegance. A swimming pool was built and the gardens improved with many ornamental flowering shrubs being planted, in which work His Royal Highness took an active part. Fort Belvedere is a name known to the nation for it was there on 11 December 1936 that Edward VIII signed the Deed of Abdication and broadcast his abdication speech. During the Second World War the Fort was taken over by the Commissioners of Crown Lands. After the war it fell into such a state of neglect and disrepair that demolition was considered. The Hon Gerald Lascelles, first cousin of HM The Queen, came to the rescue and the house was restored to its previous grandeur. One of the most attractive features of the house is that the rooms are circular, octagonal or even hexagonal – only one is rectangular.

THE CLOCKCASE *London Road 1989*

At the same time as the Shrubbs Hill Plantation was taken into Windsor Great Park, the Duke of Cumberland acquired 14 acres of Egham Common on Hangmoor Hill to the south of the Great Western Road. For this he paid the Egham vestry £5 a year in compensation. On this plot he built an observatory tower and laid out plantations of trees. From the tower the royal family might view the surrounding countryside as well as the lake. Being cut off from the rest of the park, however, the Clockcase suffered from vandalism and neglect. It was gutted by fire in 1799 and a few years later William Tough, Foreman of the Works, was warning his superiors that 'if not Repared Soon will Certainly Tumble Down'.* In 1819 it passed into private ownership and the living accommodation was improved. In the 1820s George IV, having enhanced the amenities of the lake and spending considerable time there, did not wish to be overlooked by his subjects. The Clockcase was repurchased by the Crown. It suffered arson at the hands of 'ill-disposed persons' in 1831 and this, happening at a time of rural unrest, the 'Captain Swing' riots, greatly scared the local gentry. Later in the 19th century the Clockcase was the home of a succession of royal game-keepers and royal hounds. In 1989 it remains private Crown property.

**Reproduced from Crown Copyright material in the Public Record Office Ref. CRES2/57 by permission of the Controller of Her Majesty's Stationery Office.*

VIRGINIA WATER *c.1908*

This large artificial expanse of water, that lies at the south western boundary of Windsor Great Park, was created in the early 1750s. The name Virginia pre-dates the lake, appearing as the name of a dwelling in the Egham burial register of 1656 and on a 1662 map of Windsor Great Park. To create the lake, the Bourne or Virginia River was dammed up and the natural swampy basin allowed to fill. According to tradition the digging of the first lake was carried out by William, Duke of Cumberland's soldiers. He was reluctant to disband them after they had served him faithfully in the Scottish campaign and in the Low Countries. There was also the advantage that the men in his pay could be quickly returned to military duties should the need arise. The digging and landscaping by Cumberland's men, being contained within the park pales, made little impact on the local population. The events of 1768 were different. During a late summer thunderstorm the dam holding back the waters of the first lake, burst and the water rushed down to Thorpe and Chertsey causing considerable damage. The subsequent flooding was deeply imprinted on the imagination of the men who experienced it and the inhabitants of Chertsey were fearful of it happening again.

THE CASCADE *Virginia Water c.1900*

The lake, or what was left of it, was tidied, made safe and forgotten for a decade or so. It was not until George III began to spend more time at Windsor that there was talk of 'restoring an ancient Piece of Water'. For this purpose waste land of the Manor of Egham and small properties at Egham Wick were acquired, the boundary of Windsor Great Park extended and the Great Western Road diverted. The 'Pond Head' was to be much higher than previously, height being considered the characteristic beauty of a cascade. The stones for its construction were brought from Bagshot Heath and carefully assembled. The largest were set up on the south side to form a cavern. Tons of earth were moved and levelled by local labourers, earning 10 or 12s per week. At harvest time soldiers took over the work. Feeling was strong in the neighbourhood that the cascade must never again collapse and allow the lake to flood the countryside.

THE RUINS *Virginia Water c.1906*

These ruins from the ancient town of Leptis Magna, situated to the east of Tripoli in north Africa, were brought to England in about 1818 and deposited at the British Museum. Being however, hardly the quality of the Elgin Marbles, they lay unwanted for several years until George IV and his architect, Sir Jeffry Wyatville, decided to use them to romanticise a rather neglected corner of the lake near the Ascot Road. Statues, said to have been captured from the French in the Napoleonic Wars, were placed among the ruins, but when Windsor Park was opened to the public by William IV the statues were 'abused and mutilated' by visitors and so had to be removed. Today the columns, capitals and architraves of a lost civilisation still lie in incongruous disarray in English parkland, but fenced off for the public's and the ruins' protection.

THE FISHING TEMPLE *Virginia Water c.1900*

On the north side of the lake was originally a moated summer house. In the 1820s it was embellished in typically extravagent fashion by George IV. It was said by an eye-witness to be full of 'painting and gilding and fantastic carving and swinging bells, flying dragons curling their hideous tails round the flag-staff, with all the paraphernalia of oriental illumination.' The interior walls were covered with hand-painted Chinese paper and furnished with canework and bamboo. From the lake-side balcony His Majesty would fish and then join his guests at elaborate picnic parties. Tents, including the magnificent richly ornamented example, once belonging to Tipoo Sultan and taken at the seige of Seringapatam in 1799 by Colonel Wellesley, later the Duke of Wellington, were set up in the meadow nearby. In Queen Victoria's reign the Fishing Temple was rebuilt and emerged in style like a Swiss chalet, sometimes described as the Fishing Cottage. William IV opened the south western banks of the lake to the public but the northern bank remained private. The Fishing Temple continued to be used for royal parties by Queen Victoria and her successor, Edward VII.

ROYAL SHOOTING PARTY *Virginia Water c.1908*

This group was probably taken outside the Fishing Temple. The King of Sweden, Gustav V, had only come to the throne in 1907, his queen, seated next to him being Margaret, daughter of Prince Arthur, 1st Duke of Connaught, third son of Queen Victoria. Queen Margaret's sister, later to be Lady Patricia Ramsay, is on the extreme left in the centre row. Their brother Arthur, standing at the back, married Princess Alexandra, Duchess of Fife, who in the 1940s after Prince Arthur's death lived in Hill Lodge in Wellington Avenue. Prince Alexander of Teck, seated on the extreme left, married, in 1904, Princess Alice, daughter of Prince Leopold, Queen Victoria's fourth son. Prince Alexander later became the 1st Earl of Athlone. Even in such recent times as the early 1930s Edward, Prince of Wales, later King Edward VIII, entertained at the Fishing Temple particularly in Ascot week. The building was demolished in about 1935.

VIRGINIA WATER *1908*

January 1908 was particularly cold and Virginia Water residents, as in other severe winters, took full advantage of the opportunity to skate and play hockey on the frozen lake, where once only royalty had played. *The King Edward VII,* formerly known as *Prince Eddy's Brig* is shown ice-bound. A table from the ship survives in Sunningdale Church. The brig was the latest in a long line of royal vessels kept on the lake, starting with the Duke of Cumberland's Chinese yacht, *Mandarin.* In the 1930s the tradition was continued by Edward, Prince of Wales, later King Edward VIII, who drove speed-boats on the lake.

Photographer: William End

PORTNALL *Portnall Drive c.1875*

The western corner of old Egham parish, Portnall hamlet, belonged in medieval times to the nunnery of Broomhall. In the 15th century its 90 acres and two main houses were leased to John Raynold and John Bartilmew of Egham. They claimed the freehold and sold the estate to Edward IV who emparked it. Soon, however, it returned to waste land and as such was granted to Sir William Fitzwilliam, later Earl of Southampton, who paid one rose annually for the privilege. A succession of tenant farmers worked the land. In the 18th century it was a pawn in numerous financial games, but still wheat, rye, clover and turnips were grown, trees coppiced and peat dug. In 1795 the estate came into the possession of the Reverend Thomas Bisse who found an old L-shaped house in ruinous condition. This he pulled down and built himself the three-storeyed house which still exits as the centre section of the much enlarged house in the picture. In 1817 by a deed of gift, the Reverend Thomas Bisse made over the estate of Portnall Park to his son, baptised Thomas Chaloner (with one l). Thomas later obtained permission to add the name, Challoner (with two l's) to his surname. Challoner was the name of his wife's aunt and presumed benefactress.

PORTNALL PARK *the terrace c.1890*

In 1828 Challoner returned from extensive travels on the continent to claim his inheritance and it is probable that the western wing of the mansion was built then to house the many art treasures that he brought back from Italy. A long gravel terrace extended from this gallery, a fine setting for marble seats and statues. He further landscaped the grounds and created the two artificial lakes which survive between Portnall Rise and West Drive. Having served briefly with the Dragoons and later with the Surrey Militia he was known during his time at Portnall by the name and title of Colonel Thomas Chaloner Bisse Challoner.

COL CHALONER BISSE CHALLONER *1791-1872*

Under Colonel Challoner's direction the regime at Portnall Park was strict but fair. If one of the farm labourers on the estate left his machinery out in the field he would find it padlocked on his return, and would have to go to the master for the key and to make his excuses. Challoner was an extremely orderly man himself, concerned that shoe brushes should not be in the same room as clothes brushes. Thomas's first wife, Anne, died in 1857 and two years later he married Henrietta De Salis. Sadly 'his much loved and loving Hadie' also died after a tragically short marriage. Challoner, a driving force in the local community, died himself, childless, in 1872. The estate was inherited by Henrietta's brother, Henry Jerome De Salis.

THE TACK ROOM AT PORTNALL *c.1895*

Coachmen when not driving coaches often ended up doing unusual jobs such as cutting the hair of the eldest son of the family, in this case that of Harry Edmund Challoner De Salis, born in 1891. This young man sadly died aged 21 in an Oxford hospital when he was a student at Exeter College. He was thrown from a horse while out hunting.

FISHING AT PORTNALL *1902*

With the arrival of Henry Jerome and Grace De Salis, the mansion became for the first time a family residence. The art gallery became the ballroom and the estate was alive with children and grandchildren riding, hunting, shooting, boating, fishing, making music and playing tennis. The two artificial lakes became the natural venue on a sunny afternoon to laze in a punt or, as seen here, to indulge in a spot of angling. It was important, however, that young ladies did not get too much sun and the one in the foreground is well protected.

HENRY JEROME AND GRACE DE SALIS *with their children at Portnall c.1890*

In the back row left to right are Eliza, who married their son, William, daughter Georgina, who married the Reverend Roe Hamilton, son Charles, who became Bishop of Taunton in 1911, son William, made a rear-admiral in 1911 and a KBE, son Cecil, who was a KCB and Chairman of Middlesex County Council 1919-24, son Rodolph, who inherited Portnall and was Chairman of the Singer Motor Co and of the Grand Junction Canal Co and Mary, who married Charles. Mary was formerly Lady Mary Parker, third daughter of the Earl and Countess of Macclesfield. Seated are Mary Drake, Henry Jerome's cousin, Henry Jerome, who died at Portnall in 1915, Grace, wife of Henry Jerome, and the Reverend Roe Hamilton, Curate of Sunningdale. Seated on the ground are Edith, who married Rodolph and Rachel, who married Cecil.

LABOURERS AT PORTNALL *1893*

Unfortunately this photograph of the outside staff at Portnall carries no details of the names or occupations of the people depicted. In 1881 the inside staff consisted of a butler, a footman, a cook, two lady's maids, three housemaids, a laundry maid and a laundry woman, a kitchen maid and a scullery maid, a domestic nurse and a wet nurse. Apart from Richard Smithers, the footman, who was born in Chertsey, none of these people were local. A number, whose places of birth are given as Oxfordshire, undoubtedly came with the De Salis family when they moved in about 1873 from Fringford near Bicester. The appropriately named Elizabeth Cook came from Lincolnshire. The Portnall estate must have been virtually self-contained. It boasted its own clerk of works, blacksmith and bricklayer. The Irish head gardener, Thomas May, had three gardeners and a gardener's labourer working for him and living on site. Coachmen and grooms lived over the coach house. Numerous farm labourers lived at the farms and lodges. There were three lodges: Portnall Lodge at the junction of Portnall Drive with the main road, a newer one to give more direct access to the house and later called Semple's Lodge after the occupant, and Heatherside Lodge at the Shrubbs Hill end of West Drive. Heatherside Lodge became part of the Wentworth estate in 1891. Like the inside staff many of the outside staff had come from Fringford. Some were local but a few, like Thomas Powell at Upper Portnall Farm, who originated from Wellingborough in Northamptonshire, came from much further afield.

GIPSIES AT PORTNALL LODGE *c.1890*

This photograph shows traditionally attired gipsy women playing a barrel-organ outside Portnall Lodge which at that time had a thatched roof. They were less welcome in other parts of the parish, particularly Knowle Grove. These 52 acres of 'pleasurable wood for the chase', were an isolated part of the Crown Estate and as such subject to depredation by poachers and vagrants. On one occasion in 1860 a woodman had caught the gipsies with their donkeys in the grove. He ordered them to leave and they threatened him, but before reinforcements could be brought the whole encampment had moved off.

PORTNALL PARK FARM *large barn 1931*

When Colonel Challoner leased land to the south of Portnall Park from Mrs Isabella Norton, this with the lands he already owned, made him a substantial farmer. He therefore needed a complex of farm buildings. These were constructed to the south west of Portnall Park and became known as Portnall Park Farm or Portnall Home Farm. Although no large farm house existed, there were several cottages for staff including one for the baillif, this post being held between 1840-60 by George Porton. Part of the complex, which included the walled fruit garden, survives today as Orchard Cottage.

PORTNALL PARK FARM *conversion of barn and farm buildings 1931*

After the purchase of the Portnall estate by W. G. Tarrant in the 1920s the farm complex remained derelict for some years until, in 1930, perhaps on a chance visit, it was sighted by Lady Enid de Chair. She decided it would convert into a desirable residence and extensive plans were drawn up for its transformation. The picture shows an early stage in the conversion with even the duck pond included in the plans.

PODENHALE *c.1933*

Lady de Chair called her new house Podenhale, taking an older version of the name Portnall. She and her family spent happy times at the house listening in the evenings to the sounds of the nightingale. Her husband, Admiral Sir Dudley de Chair, was Governor of New South Wales from 1924-30. Lady de Chair was instrumental in organising the Pageant of Runnymede in 1934 (see *The Egham Picture Book*). A notable feature of the gardens of this 1930s house was the Chinese moon gate, based on a 14th century painting shown to Lady de Chair by an official of the British Museum. Lady de Chair had restored several period houses, notably Bracknell Manor, before *Podenhale.* The conversion by architects Boniface & Huddert cost more and took longer than building a new house which Admiral de Chair would have preferred.

WENTWORTH'S *Wentworth Drive 1920*

At about the same time that the Reverend Thomas Bisse was building the basic house at Portnall, about two hundred acres of waste land to its north east came into the possession of Culling Charles Smith, an under secretary of state in the Foreign Office and later a commissioner of customs. He had married Lady Anne Fitzroy, the widowed sister of the eminent soldier who later became the Duke of Wellington. In about 1805 Smith built the crenellated mansion, now the home of Wentworth Golf Club. Part of the area was already known as Wentworth's waste after its owner, Mrs Elizabeth Wentworth, widow of Colonel Thomas Wentworth, who fought under General Wade in Flanders and accompanied him to Newcastle in 1745 against the pretender, Prince Charles Edward. Culling Charles Smith decided to keep the name, apostrophe and all. Like the rest of Virginia Water, these two hundred acres had once belonged to Chertsey Abbey. The monks and succeeding owners raised income by leasing out the land as a source of peat and wood. In the 17th century part of the land had been used by William Kitchen, landlord of the King's Head in Egham High Street, probably as a valuable source of fuel for the busy coaching inn.

RAMON CABRERA, COUNT DE MORELLA *1806-1876*

In 1854 Wentworth was bought by the Count and Countess de Morella. The Spanish soldier and the heiress of Welsh descent had met in November 1849 at the London home of the Duchess of Inverness, brought together by their fanatical devotion to the Carlist cause in the 1833-1849 Spanish wars of that name. Theirs was a whirlwind romance; they already knew much about each other through their mutual friends, the Carlist royal family. Ramon proposed five months after their first meeting and she, delighted with his fine eyes, expressive face and curling moustache, accepted. They were married within six weeks. A Roman Catholic ceremony was performed at the French Chapel in London where they were attended by Princess Beatrix and her husband Prince Juan, grandson of the old pretender, Don Carlos. The couple then proceeded to St George's Church, Hanover Square, where Mr Temple Frere conducted the Protestant ceremony.

CABRERA'S TOMB
in Virginia Water Churchyard 1989

Ramon Cabrera, Count de Morella and Marquis del Ter, was thought by the Duke of Wellington to have been one of the most brilliant guerrilla fighters of his time. In 1833, aged 27, he had declared himself on the side of Don Carlos, who was claiming the Spanish throne against his niece, the three-year-old Queen Isabella. Sixteen years of civil war ensued, with atrocities being committed on both sides. Cabrera rose rapidly through the ranks, becoming a general by the time he was 30, and accepting titles from his grateful prince. His brilliance, however, was not equalled by the leadership and the Carlists were repulsed in 1849. Cabrera fled to France and eventually to London where he was welcomed by a circle of Carlist well-wishers. Though, with his countess, he travelled extensively in Europe, he never returned to Spain and lies buried in a fenced-off section in the north west corner of the churchyard at Christ Church.

MARIANNE CATHERINE CABRERA, COUNTESS DE MORELLA *1820-1915*

Marianne Catherine Vaughan Richards was born in London in 1820, the daughter of an eminent barrister. Her mother died when she was only two years old and she was brought up by her grandfather and great-aunts. A precocious child, educated by masters from an early age, she was soon accompanying her father on circuit in England and on lengthy European journeys. She had a natural flair for languages, being fluent in French, Spanish and German. She remembered seeing several Carlist gentlemen just arrived in England when she was only 14 and two years later had read an English soldier's account of his experiences in Spain. She was deeply involved enough by 1839 to persuade her father to divert their journey to Bourges in France so that she might meet the Carlist royal family. She succeeded and thus began her love affair with the Carlist cause. Marianne's love for Ramon never faltered, though the problem of their different religious denominations soured her relationship with her eldest children.

THE GARTH HOUNDS *at Wentworth c.1910*

Because of her poor health before the birth, Marianne was allowed to bring up her fifth and youngest child, Ada, as a Protestant. This split the family. Luisa and Ramon, her first born daughter and son, were eventually excluded from Wentworth. The countess also became disillusioned with the Carlist cause and directed her fervour towards the new power in Europe, Prussia. To her immense pride, her second son, Augustus Ferdinand, joined the Prussian Army, later becoming Kammeljunker to the Kaiser. Sometimes with the count, sometimes with servants, she continued to travel widely in Europe, often seeking out the current battle sites. Her other great love was horses. She rode with the Garth Hounds, once entertaining Edward, Prince of Wales, later King Edward VII, at a Wentworth meet. Her determination to continue riding made her doctors despair. She did not give up hunting until she was 75 and riding until she was 80. For 60 years she reigned at Wentworth, for nearly 40 years a widow. She was kind to retainers, especially when they were sick. She died only five years short of her century and was buried beside her husband in Virginia Water churchyard. Her youngest daughter, Ada, inherited the estate; her two middle sons had pre-deceased her and Ramon and Luisa were ignored.

MORELLA COTTAGE *Wellington Avenue 1939*

The countess's devotion to her husband and her knowledge of his military campaigns are perpetuated in the names she gave to the houses built after his death for the Wentworth staff. All have distinctive name stones. Cabrera Cottages are in Crown Road and record the count's family name. On the corner of Crown Road and Wellington Avenue once stood Morella Cottage, seen in the photograph. It was named after the mountain town in eastern Spain that Cabrera occupied in 1838. As a result he was created Count de Morella. The cottage was pulled down in 1972 but its name stone survives in The Egham Museum. On the left of the picture is Ebro Cottage, the last to be built in 1909. The name commemorates one of the longest of Spain's rivers. Cabrera's birthplace is on its banks. It was a natural line of defence in Cabrera's Carlist wars.

Cantavieja Cottage is near Christ Church. Geographically Cantavieja, occupied by Cabrera in 1835, is a mountain town in the Maestrazgo region of eastern Spain. It became his fortress, his headquarters, his quartermaster's stores and his propaganda centre. His presence is still remembered there.

Cabrera Square in Tortosa.

Cabrera Square in Cantavieja.

Near Cantavieja Cottage is Elter Cottage, a puzzling name until one realises that the English mason charged with carving the name stone, made one English word from two Spanish. El Ter was the name of the river on the banks of which Cabrera fought his last battle on Spanish soil, the Battle of Pasteral in 1848. After this battle Cabrera was created Marquis del Ter.

A road named for Cabrera in Virginia Water.

TORTOSA COTTAGES *Trumps Green Road 1920*

Tortosa Cottages are in Trumps Green and commemorate Cabrera's birthplace, where he spent his childhood and failed as a priest. It was in this town that his mother was taken as a hostage by his enemies and in 1836 executed as a reprisal for actions taken by her son.

WENTWORTH *staff wedding 1912*

When Frank Pyne, the countess's footman, married Cathy Patterson one of the housemaids, it was a great day for the Wentworth staff. They attended in force, as elegantly dressed as for a society wedding. Behind the bride is William Cosham, for many years Wentworth's butler, with his wife on his right. On the extreme left is William Chapman, one of the estate's game-keepers. His brother John is on the right. The two small bridesmaids in the front are William's daughters, Louisa and Dorothy. The photograph was taken against a background of laurel and bamboo at Bagshot Lodge, the Chapmans' home. The lodge was situated on the Great Western Road at the end of Wentworth Drive. The bridegroom was attended by his three brothers sitting with him in the bride's row. Fellow servants and friends completed the picture.

PINEWOOD LODGE *Pinewood Road 1930s*

Bagshot Lodge, the western entrance to the old Wentworth estate, has been rebuilt. Wellington Lodge at the eastern end and Pinewood to the north survive as delightful cottages. They would have been extremely cramped for the estate families who lived there in Victorian and Edwardian times and with none of the amenities that the present age takes for granted. The heads of the family worked as game-keeper, gardener, or labourer for the countess; the wives and children would have been expected to keep an eye on the road to open gates for visitors as required. In the photograph the signpost points to the riding stables then at Wentworth Home Farm. In the Runnymede Pageant of 1934, the riding school manager, Captain E. W. Joslin, rode his horse, *Bimbo*, in the 'Masque of the Proud Horse', part of the Tudor scene. The monkey puzzle tree on the right survives.

WENTWORTH POND *off Wentworth Drive 1920*

A small dam and waterfall constructed on the Bourne near Wentworth resulted in the formation of a miniature Virginia Water of six acres. The date of construction is unknown but appears to have been in the latter half of the 19th century. In 1913 the pond was witness to a bizarre event. The Countess de Morella and her daughter, Ada, were in residence at Wentworth. The disinherited son, Ramon, desiring to secure some family discourse, sent his son, also called Ramon, a lieutenant in the Spanish army, to see the countess. She, having some inkling of the intended arrival of the lieutenant, had Sergeant Matthews of the Chertsey police in attendance. The countess indicated that Lieutenant Cabrera was not welcome. Albert Luff, the coachman, John Chapman, lodge keeper and gardener and William Paice, the agent for the estate, offered to 'escort' him off the premises. It was later said that they threatened to throw him in the pond. The lieutenant left but later summoned the three members of staff for assault. The case was heard at Chertsey court with the famous barrister, Curtis-Bennett, for the prosecution but the case was dismissed. The lieutenant died in Morocco in 1938 while in the service of General Franco. In the 1920s W. G. Tarrant arranged for the Ben Great Players to present 'As You Like It' and 'Midsummer Night's Dream' on the lawn above the pond.

BOG BRIDGE *West Drive c.1920*

The River Bourne starts in Virginia Water as two streams. One comes from the lake, the other rises in a morose kind of way over towards Longcross. They converge at a point west of Wellington Bridge in Wellington Avenue, a point described in old deeds as Clearford. The Longcross river is known locally as the 'Boggy Bourne' and in old deeds as the Redebourne. This picture shows Robert Trowbridge leaning on a fence in this rural location at about the time that W. G. Tarrant was starting his negotiations for the purchase of Wentworth. At this point the Boggy Bourne formed the boundary between the De Salis family's Portnall estate and the Cabrera family's Wentworth estate. The bridge still exists in West Drive rebuilt for the traffic of today.

W. G. TARRANT *and his staff c.1922*

W. G. Tarrant started his own business in Byfleet in 1895, first as a carpenter and later as a builder. He soon established a reputation for high quality materials and workmanship. In 1920 after the failure of the auction sale, Tarrant bought the Wentworth estate from Miss Ada Cabrera. He planned it, like his earlier development, St George's Hill, Weybridge, to be the ideal place for the business or professional man to live, where the natural beauty of the area would be preserved and there would be excellent facilities for golf and tennis. The first Tarrant house on Wentworth, *Weather Heath,* was built in 1923 and Wentworth Club formed in 1924. 'WG' built a house for himself, *Eastfield* in Woodlands Road West, a road originally intended to be called 'Copse Road' and to be a through road with what became Woodlands Road East. He lived there until 1931. He played the organ at Christ Church, sang in the choir and ran a choral society at Wentworth. The sign of a Tarrant-built house is a monogram of his initials carved in stone, usually in the wall by the main entrance. A good example may be seen on the front wall of Barclays Bank, Station Approach. Mr Tarrant is seen seated 9th from the left in the front row, and his right hand man at Wentworth, Cecil James Croucher, 6th from the left.

MONKS ROAD *c.1932*

In the 1930s photographers would make a postcard out of almost anything. Here the partially developed Monks Road is described as Wentworth Estate. Plots were marked out in the former 20-acre arable field of Trotsworth Farm at an early stage in the development. To remind us that in medieval times the land had been in monastic hands the new roads were called Monks Road, Abbey Road and Nuns Walk. By 1939, 359 houses had been built on the Wentworth Estate as a whole.

LITTLEWOOD *a typical Tarrant house, built 1924*

Weather Heath and *Littlewood* were the first two houses to be built on the estate, the former having stabling for four horses. Every attempt was made in the design and building of the houses to set them into the landscape and the larger houses usually had plots of several acres. Tarrant was determined that the estate should not be monotonous. In a number of cases eminent architects were employed. This has meant that in recent years, some 50 years on, several Wentworth houses have been 'listed' by the Department of the Environment as of historic interest. In this picture *Littlewood* is seen as originally built, when the owner was Joseph Telford Quick. The little dormer windows and the loggia were typical Tarrant features.

LITTLEWOOD *1989*

Very few Tarrant houses retain all their original features. The style of this house has moved with the times. The brick has been rendered, the gables altered and the windows enlarged. An extension has been made on the left and where there was formerly a lawn is now an attractive swimming pool.

GOLF AT WENTWORTH

Pam Barton at Wentworth 1935

In 1920 after she had inherited Wentworth from her mother and after the objections to her mother's will by her elder brother and sister had been resolved, Ada Cabrera decided to put Wentworth up for sale. The estate was divided up into 46 lots and an elaborate sale catalogue produced. Unfortunately, owing probably to the state of the economy in Britain after the First World War, there were very few takers when the sale took place on 27 May 1920. W. G. Tarrant, the Byfleet builder, however, purchased the remaining lots. Having already developed the golf course at St George's Hill, Weybridge, 'WG' set about repeating his ideas at Wentworth. The East Course was laid out by the well known golf architect, Harry S. Colt, and Wentworth Club formed in 1924. Colt's excellent work and the attractive surroundings soon brought the international golfing scene to Wentworth and in 1932 the Curtis Cup match was played there. The Americans won the cup for the first time. In this picture ex-Curtis Cup player, Pam Barton, of the Royal Mid-Surrey Golf Club is seen competing in the London Ladies Foursomes at Wentworth. Sadly she died in 1940 as the result of an aeroplane crash.

GOLF AT WENTWORTH

The Canada Cup Match 1956

This picture shows the first televising of an outside golf tournament by the BBC and the very primitive scaffolding which held the cameras and microphone for sound effects. The hole is the 7th on the West Course, also laid out by H. S. Colt. The 9th fairway and Chobham Common in the background are clearly visible, a view which today is totally obscured by trees. The course was said to have been groomed to perfection and the Club secretary and the stewards received high praise for the magnificent organisation. The event was run on a scale not before seen on this side of the Atlantic. During the Second World War a concrete road, to join Chobham Lane with Longcross Station, was built for the military, who christened it 'The Burma Road', a name now officially assigned to it. As a result of the proximity of this road to the West Course the name has become translated and the West Course has become known to golfers as 'The Burma Road'. There are other later versions of this story. Golfing stars from 29 countries participated in this match.

GOLF AT WENTWORTH

The Piccadilly World Match Play Tournament 1965

This picture shows the attractive woodland setting of the Wentworth courses. Since the 1950s viewing sport on television has become a national pastime and there must be few who have not seen some of the world matches that have become annual Wentworth events. Here we see the crowd following Arnold Palmer of the USA and Kel Nagle of Australia across the fairway in the 1965 Piccadilly World Match Play Tournament.

GOLF AT WENTWORTH

The Piccadilly World Match Play Tournament 1967

Arnold Palmer of the USA beat Peter Thomson of Australia by one hole. Here the players are seen walking down the 33rd fairway followed by the large gallery. The crowds were then controlled by ropes held by stewards, whereas today each fairway is lined with stakes and ropes at tournament time. The gentleman to the right of the score board is the late Gerald Micklam, past member and Captain of Sunningdale Golf Club.

LUDDINGTON HOUSE *Stroude Road 1989*

This well proportioned house on the borders of Egham and Stroude was built by a mysterious Gironomo of the household of James II. It was enlarged and improved in the 18th century by Richard Wyatt from Nynehead in Somerset. His beautiful daughters and cultural interests helped to make the house a social and artistic centre. In 1765, his son, also Richard, married Priscilla Edgell and eventually became master of her inheritance, Milton Park. At the end of the 18th century Luddington was bought by Walter Irvine of the Island of Tobago. He, 'having amassed a splendid fortune in the West Indies', brought his young wife to Luddington where their four children were born. Their only son died in infancy; their youngest daughter also died young. Their eldest daughter, Elizabeth, married into the Douglas family, while the middle daughter, Christina, remained at Luddington House all the 71 years of her life. Most of the Irvine family are buried in Egham Parish Church, but Christina lies in a tomb near the door of the church she and her mother endowed in Virginia Water.

STROUDE CHAPEL *Stroude Road c.1908*

Christina Irvine of Luddington House dedicated herself to charitable works. In 1826 two schools were listed in Stroude as being supplied and maintained by 'the private bounty' of Miss Irvine and her neighbour at Milton Park, Edgell Wyatt Edgell. She was at the same time planning to build a school at St Ann's Heath to which Mr Edgell would also contribute. For many years in the 19th century a school was held in the little Church Room pictured here. In 1908 the trustees of Holloway Sanatorium purchased the Church Room and the two adjoining cottages for £500 and divine service was conducted in the Church Room by the Reverend John Peck, Chaplain of the sanatorium. The Church Room continued to be used for prayer meetings and Sunday School until the electricity was found to be unsafe. In 1985 it was incorporated into the neighbouring cottage, once lived in by Walter Busby, the chimney sweep at the sanatorium.

CHRIST CHURCH *Virginia Water*
1955 above   1927 right

In 1830-31 riots swept through most of the counties of southern England, incidents of incendiarism being reported at Englefield Green and at the Clockcase. Such unrest made the ruling classes fearful of revolution. One way of maintaining 'a degree of good order' in society was to reclaim the backsliding poor into the established church. Few Virginia Water inhabitants, it would seem, regularly walked the three or so miles to the new church in Egham, its fine neo-classic design and private pews intimidating rather than welcoming them. In March 1837, therefore, the Egham vestry was delighted to be informed that Christina Irvine, 'a pious and benevolent female inhabitant' wished to give £2,000 in free gift for the endowment of a church for the labouring poor in Virginia Water. Christina had already devoted much energy to good works and her motives would seem to have been charitable and spiritual rather than political. The site at the intersection of the Chobham and Chertsey roads, now Callow Hill and Christchurch Road was donated by Mrs Elizabeth Irvine, Christina's mother. The total cost of the building, £2,019, was met by public subscription, the young Queen Victoria heading the list, followed by the local landowners.

Photograph above: Robert Walker

CHRIST CHURCH *interior view c.1955*

The architect was William Fuller Pocock of Glenridge, Callow Hill. A devout Methodist he offered his services free. The interior was designed to be simple, with a minimum of paid pews. Just before consecration day a severe storm struck: two of the pinnacles were blown down, damaging the tiling and plastering. The architect complained that the pinnacles had been incorrectly attached and the builders, Northcrofts of Egham, were quickly summoned to do the repairs. Christ Church was consecrated on the appointed day – 3 November 1838 – by the Bishop of Winchester, Charles Richard Sumner. The finished church was grander than had been originally planned. Because of the favourable state of the finances a tower and a spire were added and Culling Charles Smith of Wentworth's donated the clock. The pinnacles remained a distinctive feature of the church until the late 1950s when they were removed for safety reasons. Inside the church, above the reredos, the theme of the pinnacles was repeated. Over the years the population of Virginia Water has changed and grown, the congregation of Christ Church likewise. In the early 1980s an ambitious extension was planned, a Church Centre to adjoin the eastern wall of the church with sliding doors. In 1985 it was completed, enabling the church itself to expand for the great festivals and accommodating under one roof many facets of the church community. At the same time the pulpit and gallery were removed and the pews replaced by chairs. One of the pews which included a seat for the priest was given to The Egham Museum.

Photographer: Robert Walker

CHRIST CHURCH VICARAGE *c.1955*

In August 1838 the Egham vestry agreed that land should be set aside for a clergyman's house and garden. Part of Miss Irvine's endowment was used for that purpose. The Reverend Thomas Page, previously a curate at Egham Parish Church, became Virginia Water's first vicar. As a member of the committee that steered Christ Church into being, he was given the task of soliciting subscriptions from both Virginia Water and Egham worthies. He too became the victim of 'evil-disposed persons' when he was shot at through the vicarage window in the summer of 1843. Fortunately he suffered no injury. This delightful vicarage became too difficult and expensive to maintain and it was demolished in the late 1960s.

Photographer: Robert Walker

CHRIST CHURCH SCHOOL
Christchurch Road 1982

Among the fitments for the new church were two benches for the schoolmistresses. The Sunday school was, from the beginning, a vital part of the new ministry. By 1843 with 70 boys and 60 girls attending Sunday School, the Reverend Thomas Page felt justified in applying to the National Society for help and advice on establishing a Church of England day school. He stressed the generosity of his parishioners in subscribing towards the building of the church, even though 'only two wealthy families and three respectable farmers' resided in Virginia Water. The money was raised in record time. The school was completed within a year, built on land donated by St George Caulfield, then of Wentworth's. His little daughter, Emily aged 10, laid the foundation stone. The school opened in December 1843 with 103 children on its register. In 1939, with only 15 pupils attending, Christ Church School was about to close. The arrival of wartime evacuees and the postwar baby and building boom saved it. Today it is a flourishing CE First School.

SCHOOL PUPILS *at Christ Church School c.1908*

The visit of the photographer was an annual event at the Virginia Water school in the 19th and early 20th centuries. The pupils were reminded to appear at school especially tidily dressed for the photograph, boys in brushed suits and well polished shoes, the girls in clean pinafores. On this occasion Louisa and Dorothy Chapman, daughters of the countess's game-keeper at Bagshot Lodge, rebelled. They can be seen sitting in the second row, looking remarkably alike in their red smocked dresses, the collars edged with lace. They had decided to sneak to school in their best dresses, and not to wear pinafores on the great day. Two assistant teachers, Mrs Hubbard on the left and Miss Banks on the right, posed with the children.

SCHOOLMASTER'S HOUSE *Christ Church School c.1919*

As was often the custom in the 19th century the schoolmaster or mistress lived on site in a house adjoining the school. In the first 30 years of the school's existence the house was mostly occupied by married couples, once by a brother and sister, who shared the teaching. From 1874 until recent times unmarried schoolmistresses ran Christ Church School, experiencing rather lonely lives, alone in the schoolhouse. In fact the house was regarded as being so isolated that during the First World War many women refused the appointment. Miss Hilda Lyle, seen here outside the schoolhouse, accepted because she had friends in the parish. The Egham School Board was reluctant to appoint her as she had insufficient certificated experience. With the support, however, of the vicar of the time, the Reverend Molyneux, and the National Society she came to Virginia Water. The last headteacher to live in the schoolhouse was Edith Hooker who retired in 1964. In 1989 the schoolhouse is about to become a library and resource centre.

GARDENING AT CHRIST CHURCH SCHOOL *1914-1918*

Pupils are seen here playing their part in the production of food in the First World War. Virginia Water's country children were quite used to self sufficiency; most cottage gardens were big enough for a large vegetable patch; hedgerows produced fruit and nuts, heathland wood and acorns; chickens were kept and even as late as 1921 some cottages on Callow Hill still had pig-sties.

GLENRIDGE *Callow Hill c.1925*

The Inclosure Act of 1814 changed the character of Callow Hill. Large and small plots were carved out of the waste, cottages and gentlemen's houses were built. At that time it was becoming more and more popular for London gentlemen to escape from town for the summer. The faster coach roads even made it possible for them to return to London on Monday morning after spending weekends at their country retreats. In 1823, the London architect, William Fuller Pocock, liking what he saw of the neighbourhood, bought 'a few acres of Heath land' at Callow Hill. He designed and built a small cottage on the site, his two young sons laying the first bricks. The family spent many summers there enjoying a simple rural life. Over the years rooms and floors were added so that by the time William's second son, Thomas Wilmer Pocock, was in residence the little cottage had become a mansion. From the 1920s it was run as an hotel, 'a charming old English Country House – with excellent cuisine'. In the 1970s it was in a ruinous state and in a few years demolished. Virginia Beeches now stands on the site.

THE ROSE AND OLIVE BRANCH *Callow Hill 1937*

By 1851 Callow Hill, with more cottages having been built, also had it own beerhouse, originally the Rose. It was run by Robert Hart of Chertsey, who had come to Virginia Water to work at Trotsworth Farm. In 1847 he married Mary Ann Beauchamp, shop-keeper of Callow Hill. They soon acquired the necessary licence and sold beer as well as groceries. It is possible that the house was previously occupied by Mary Ann's father, John Beauchamp, for as well as looking after her own little family she took charge of two younger brothers and an invalid sister. In May 1937, like numerous other public houses throughout the country, the Rose and Olive Branch put up celebratory flags and bunting in honour of the coronation of HM King George VI and HM Queen Elizabeth. The hop leaf sign of Simonds, the Reading brewer, is to be seen hanging above the doorway.

KENWOLDE COURT *Callow Hill 1920*

In the key to the Poor Law Map of 1856 two unfinished houses are listed on land belonging to Streatfield, Lawrence and Mortimore who at that time owned Trotsworth Farm including the brickworks just off Hollow Lane. By 1860 Thomas Lawrence was occupying the house later known as Merlewood and William Mortimore the one then called Trotsworth House and later Kenwolde. Within a year or two both properties, together with the rest of the Manor of Trotsworth, were in the hands of the Count and Countess de Morella. Until the mid 1870s they leased Kenwolde to Mrs Mary Vizard, an elderly widow, who with her unmarried step-daughter, Caroline, took an immediate interest in church and school. Over the years other tenants enjoyed the 15 or so acres of gardens, pleasure grounds, tennis courts, croquet lawn and, a particular feature, a pretty elliptical rose garden. Inside, included in the fine reception rooms on the ground floor, were a library and a billiard room. Kenwolde continued to be a gentleman's residence after it was offered for sale as part of the Wentworth estate in 1920. Major Ellis George Whately lived there in the 1930s and 40s. In about 1950 it was bought by the London County Council and opened as an old people's home. In the early 1980s it was converted into three separate houses.

MERLEWOOD *Hollow Lane 1920*

Like Kenwolde, Merlewood was built of buff-coloured brick which, it would be pleasant to imagine, came from the Trotsworth brickworks. Again like Kenwolde, Merlewood was acquired by the Count and Countess de Morella in the early 1860s. They leased it to Charles Pilgrim, who, with his wife and widowed sister, Sarah Borrer, became even more involved in local affairs than his neighbour, Mrs. Vizard. To care for the house and its three elderly occupants, a butler, a footman, a cook, two lady's maids, a housemaid and a kitchen maid were in residence. The estate was more spacious than Kenwolde's, comprising 24 acres of pleasure gardens, orchards, gardens, glasshouses, a fish pond and half an acre of ornamental water where once withies had grown. The gardener lived at the lodge, now a separate residence, while the coachman and his wife lived over the stable. In 1913 Donald Macmaster rented the house for a few years while he was the local member of parliament. In about 1928 Merlewood passed into the hands of the Smith family until in about 1950 it was acquired by The Distressed Gentlefolks' Association.

CALLOW HILL SANDPIT *1920s*

Edgell Wyatt Edgell of Milton Park owned many acres of land in and around Egham in the mid 19th century. In about 1852 he embarked on an extensive tree-planting programme. Having completed the work he decided to have a stone cut to commemorate the occasion. This stone was installed on Callow Hill. However, Callow Hill was found to have a rather useful outcrop of sand which was worked in the 1920s by Tarrant as this picture shows. Wyatt Edgell's stone obviously had to be removed but when and by whom is not known. It was found by members of Egham-by-Runnymede Historical Society near Egham Library in the early 1980s. Through the generosity of Johnson Wax Ltd the stone was restored in 1985 and erected in the grounds of Milton Park, it being impractical to re-install it at Callow Hill. A plaque was put alongside it telling its story. The stone and plaque are sited so that the public can see them near the roundabout in Stroude Road. After the sand had been extracted, the Callow Hill site was popular as the location for several films, notably *Stranglers of Bombay* in 1959. Then it became a rubbish dump, London waste being brought down in Drinkwater lorries, gigantic for their time. Callow Hill residents were relieved when the filling was complete and the area sown with grass. In the photograph are four of the sandpit workers: Robert Trowbridge, who then lived at Cabrera Cottages, is second from the left; on the extreme right is Jim Smithers who lived in Hollow Lane, in Gorse Hill Cottage, now demolished.

WELLINGTON AVENUE *looking north c.1930*

In earlier times roads were named straightforwardly after the places they linked. Thus Wellington Avenue was the Chobham and Windsor Road. As such it led from Clearford, now Wellington Bridge, past Warren Farm to pick up the present Chobham Lane to the south. Early in the 19th century the road was re-aligned to link with the hamlet of Knowle Hill. After the Napoleonic Wars, when the victory at Waterloo was still vivid in people's minds it seemed appropriate to name the new road after the Duke of Wellington. It commemorated not only a national hero, but also a local visitor, for the Duke's widowed sister, Lady Ann Fitzroy, had married Culling Charles Smith of Wentworth's, and the Iron Duke must have ridden along the road named after him. The Wentworth estate lay to the left of the photograph. Callow Hill is straight ahead. Before 1814 the area round Callow Hill was part of Egham Common, used by local inhabitants for grazing animals or wooding.

THE STAG AND HOUNDS BEERHOUSE

Wellington Avenue c.1900

The Beerhouse Act of 1830 enabled certain householders to sell beer in their own houses at the cost of two guineas a year for an excise licence. In 1841 the widow, Hannah Staples, and her son Joseph, an 'Assistant at the Barrier', held the licence. The family with the longest association with the Stag and Hounds was, however, the Broom family. Samuel Broom came from Norfolk some time in the early 1840s, became one of Egham's first police constables, married a local girl and eventually took over a small beerhouse in Egham Fields. He must have prospered for he soon owned several cottages at Knowle Hill. In 1881 he moved to the Stag and Hounds with his second wife and young family. His fourth daughter, Winifred, was a particularly bright pupil at Christ Church School and became a teacher. The licence of the beerhouse passed to Mrs Isabella Broom after her husband's death. It is possible that she is in the centre of the photograph. The house was then taken over by Isabella's daughter, Amy, and son-in-law, Robert James Hammond. During their tenancy, in about 1922, the old beerhouse was pulled down.

HAWTHORN COTTAGE *Wellington Avenue c.1975*

The 1790 Survey of the Parish of Egham shows a small community in the Knowle Hill area, both on Clod Hill itself, as it is locally known; and at the southern end of Wellington Avenue. By 1881 it was a self contained community, a blacksmith, a carpenter, a woodfencer, a shepherd, a game-keeper, a carter, a painter as well as gardeners and labourers residing there. It also boasted a grocer's shop. Hawthorn Cottage, the cottage in the photograph, may well have been one of the original settlements. Inside was a kitchen with a small portable range, a pantry and three bedrooms each with a fireplace. At the rear was a woodshed and a wash-house with copper and sink but even as late as 1920 all water had to be carried from the well shared with Woodbine Cottages next door. Hawthorn Cottage was pulled down in 1981 and three houses built on the site.

Photographer: Jane Burn

TRUMPS GREEN FARM *Lyne Road 1989*

At the end of the 18th century Andrew Mackason, an Egham butcher, purchased Trumps Green Farm from David Saker probably as an investment. The property, originally called Elmers, consisted of a farmhouse and 26 acres of land distributed over about 10 nearby fields. It eventually passed to his two grand-daughters, Louisa and Mary Woolhouse. Some of the land was sold to the Staines, Wokingham and Woking Junction Railway and as a result Trumps Green was cut in half. The pond, which is still just about visible, ended up on the south side of the railway line; the beerhouse, the Crown, was left on the north side and only a footpath remains to connect the two halves of the old hamlet. By 1881 when Thomas Land, a retired civil servant, purchased the property for £500 little more than two acres remained. The land was let to James Page and James Godfrey, one of whom may have occupied the farmhouse. In 1883 Land's widow, Annie, was described as living at The Knowle. Fortunately Trumps Green farmhouse survives as an attractive residence.

THE CROWN BEERHOUSE
Trumps Green Road c.1905

This cottage was first mentioned as a beerhouse in the census return for 1851, but the building was in existence earlier, owned and occupied by William Jennings in 1790. Its first licensee, Henry Brooker, combined this job with shoe-making, his wife Harriet being a shoe-binder. It was not uncommon for beerhouse keepers to have second jobs. In 1892 the Crown was owned by Friary Holroyd & Co, the Guildford brewers, and described in a record of licensed premises as catering 'for the respectable working class'. It is possible that the present Crown public house was built around this old cottage; it is certainly on the same site.

VIRGINIA WATER STATION ENTRANCE *c.1905*

The railway reached Virginia Water in 1856 when the Staines, Wokingham & Woking Junction Railway joined Staines to Ascot and to Wokingham on the South Eastern Railway. Depite the objections of Colonel Challoner who thought the railway would bring the wrong kind of people down from London, a station was built at Virginia Water. Originally it was thought the station would be called Trotsworth. It was variously called 'Virginia Water for Chertsey and Weybridge' and 'Virginia Water for Wentworth'. This photograph shows the rural nature of the entrance to the station before the era of the golf club and the London commuter. The wide carriage road in the foreground which could be closed off, has been eliminated by a car park and the site of the war memorial. The road bridge originally had no pavement. The bridge was closed to traffic for a short period at the end of the Second World War following structural damage caused by heavy military vehicles crossing it. In the 1960s a foot bridge was installed on the London side but removed in the 1970s when the road bridge was extensively rebuilt and widened.

VIRGINIA WATER STATION *c.1926*

When the London & South Western Railway decided to make Chertsey a through station from 1866, rather than a terminal branch off their main line, their line was joined to the Reading line at Virginia Water which thus became a junction. For many years Virginia Water had three signalboxes – one centrally placed, as seen here, between platforms 2 and 3 and one at each end of the western curve which joined the Weybridge and Reading lines and allowed direct running between Weybridge and Reading. This was, however, little used and the track was taken up, although the writer recalls travelling round it and alighting at Longcross in the 1960s during engineering work. The small shelter on the central platform looks only towards the Reading line and probably pre-dates the Weybridge branch.

VIRGINIA WATER STATION *c.1972*

This photograph was taken shortly before the demolition of the original station buildings. This attractive and substantial building was replaced by a prefabricated type modern structure. The VR letter box which is seen here in the wall near the entrance to platform 1 is now in The Egham Museum. There was formerly a three bay siding on the Reading line at the west side of the station, mainly used for coal traffic by Drake & Mount, whose coal order office is now the office of Baker's taxi service. The footpath from Trumps Green originally approached the station at a higher level and it was necessary to cross the sidings to reach the station entrance. Holloway Sanatorium had a coal siding from which through a tunnel, coal was moved into the building.

VIRGINIA WATER STATION *platform 3 c.1920*

For a long time the Staines to Weybridge service was operated by 'motor trains' – push pull services avoiding the need to change the engine to the front of the train. Here an Adams T1 0-4-4T engine of 1888-96 in LSWR livery is pushing a two-car coach set towards Staines. These engines were scrapped by British Railways in the early 1950s. Electrification came to the Weybridge line in 1937 and was operated mostly by two-car NOL units with wooden bodies. After a disastrous fire at Barnes in 1955 when a number of local people, including the tennis star, Bernard Crouch, were killed, the wooden stock was scrapped. For years after electrification passengers to Weybridge pondered on why the train waited several minutes at Chertsey, little realising this wait had been left in the timetable from the days of steam and was intended for the locomotive to pick up water. The Reading line was electrified in 1939. In the 1960s before modernisation and before steam finally disappeared, the magnificent coal fires in the three waiting rooms at Virginia Water, tended by the redoubtable Fred Williams, kept many a commuter warm.

Photographer: H. C. Casserley

VIRGINIA WATER STATION *rose-garden c.1913*

At the beginning of the 20th century Alfred Smith was station master at Virginia Water station and therefore lived at Station House. He loved roses. James S. Ogilvy in *A Pilgrimage in Surrey* wrote enthusiastically of the scene: 'roses on the signal posts, on the fences, the railway banks – roses everywhere.' The air was perfumed with their scent. In the photograph Mr Smith is seen amidst his roses on the bank by platform 4. Mr Ogilvy also noted 'the torrent of children in many coloured garments, freed from excursion trains, toddling down the long mile of road leading to their paradise of water, wood, bracken, and heather:' Virginia Water.

VIRGINIA WATER STATION *platform staff 1930s*

Like all country stations in the 1920s and 1930s Virginia Water always had plenty of staff on the platforms. William Coy, seated left, and Dick Stephens, third from the left, were two of the porters. With four platforms to attend to and two entrances at which to take tickets there was always plenty to do. Although the small goods yard only handled coal there was a busy trade in parcels by passenger train and passenger's luggage in advance. A van called daily to pick these up and to deliver them locally. The three signalboxes also needed numerous staff to maintain shifts. One of the signalmen is seated on the extreme right. The station master in the 1930s was Mr Vernon Toze.

THE RAILWAY HOTEL *Christchurch Road c.1905*

In 1856 the licensee of the Wheatsheaf inn planned to extend his accommodation in anticipation of the increased trade that the railway would bring to the district. This did not preclude a public house being built at 'Trotsworth' station but there were no immediate plans for a station hotel. Indeed the Railway Tavern did not open until about 1873. It was owned by Neville Reid, the Windsor brewers, and run by John Evered Poole and his wife with the help of four resident staff: a barmaid, a housemaid and an 'odd man' and his wife. By the time J. Coulson took over in the 1890s the Railway was not only a hotel but a posting house; it had good hotel and stabling accommodation as well as a 'respectable bar trade' and a billiard room. The many visitors to Holloway Sanatorium must have found the ready availability of luncheons and teas and the private sitting rooms particularly attractive. The Railway Hotel changed its name to the Trottesworth in about 1967 and now boasts two restaurants and a barbecue marquee.

OLD WOODSIDE *Christchurch Road c.1920*

This delightful house stood back from the road where Woodside Close now is. For many years up to the 1940s it was occupied by Mark Hill, the manager of Drake & Mount's coal depot at Virginia Water. The house had three sitting rooms, two kitchens as well as a wash house and cellar. There were four main bedrooms with a smaller one and a boxroom for the use of domestic staff. Stabling, orchard, pasture and arable land made up its three acres. In the 1920 auction catalogue its land was said to be 'of a fertile character'. This was important for John William Ellis, a gardener at Great Fosters, when he built his house, *Indiana,* and established a business as landscape gardener and nurseryman on part of the site in the early 1930s. When his sons returned from war service in 1945 they were desirous of expanding the business but this was not possible and they eventually moved to Worplesdon. By 1960 old Woodside and a newer house on the same site were empty and planning permission had been obtained for Woodside Close.

SUNNINGDALE STATION *1856*

Like Virginia Water, Sunningdale station opened in 1856. The level crossing must be one of few that straddle a major trunk road. The goods sidings have disappeared under Waitrose's car park. The station was completely remodelled in the 1970s, the earlier buildings being demolished. The signal box became redundant in 1975 when remote controlled barriers replaced the gates.

ST AGNES CHURCH *Sunningdale 1985*

Sunningdale was established as a village in the 19th century. Nearby Sunninghill is a much older settlement. Sunningdale is in three parts; two are in Surrey, one in the Borough of Runnymede, and the other in the Borough of Surrey Heath; the third part, containing the parish church, is in Berkshire. St Agnes mission church, made of corrugated iron, was in Halfpenny Lane, off Chobham Road, until about two years after this picture was taken when the site was sold for building and the church demolished. The nave of the church was in Surrey Heath while the altar was in Runnymede. The altar was presented to the church in 1913 by Frederica Swinburne in memory of her mother, Hannah Entwisle. The front of the altar contains a panel depicting the Annunciation, painted after the style of Giotto. The altar is now in The Egham Museum. A stained glass east window, formerly in the London Mothers' Home in Chobham Road, was removed from St. Agnes Church before demolition and installed in Sunningdale Parish Church.

BROOMFIELD HALL *Sunningdale c.1905*

Broomfield Hall was probably built for the Reverend Joshua Hird, the first incumbent of the newly formed parish of Sunningdale. In 1845 at the young age of 35, Joshua Hird died leaving a widow and several children. Three years later his widow, Elizabeth, married Captain Joseph Dingwall at Christ Church, Virginia Water. In 1869 Dingwall made a train journey to London from Sunningdale station. Thomas Holloway, who happened to be in the same carriage, overheard Dingwall say that he had thought of selling Broomfield. Holloway immediately offered £25,000 for the house and contents which was accepted. In Holloway's own words 'it was all done in a quarter of an hour.' Dingwall moved to St Servan in France for a while and later to Turkey where he died at Mersina in 1873.

Photographer: William End

BROOMFIELD HALL

remains of the coach house and stables 1989

All that remain of Broomfield are the lodge, now used as an estate agent's office, and the coach house and stables, the lower floor of which is now occupied by shops. Holloway pulled down most of the original house and engaged a Mr Nutt of Camden Town to build in its place 'a mansion suitable for a gentleman of fortune'. However, Holloway apparently did not want to live in the final result and sold it in 1872 to James Reiss for £20,000. Mr Reiss made further alterations. His initials remain on a shield at the rear of the coach house tower. Holloway stored Dingwall's furniture and collection of pictures in a remaining room in the old hall and in the coach house. These included paintings by van Dijk, Rubens and David and Bellini's 'St Francis in Ecstasy'. The latter painting is now in the Frick collection in New York. Holloway kept the collection intact and installed them in the billiard room of his house, *Tittenhurst,* in Sunninghill. The last owner of Broomfield was Alexandre Chevallier. In 1930-31 it was pulled own and the site built upon.

WALNUT TREE COTTAGE *Stroude c.1933*

In the mid-19th century Stroude was, as it had been for centuries, a small self-contained community of about 16 households. It had its own shop and beerhouse, its own craftsmen and its own farms, market gardens and nearby gentlemen's estates to provide work. Its early houses would have been timber framed like the one in the picture; Surrey had plenty of wood. A large walnut tree is visible on the right of the picture and local children were skilled at gathering the nuts. Walnut Tree Cottage was occupied in the 20th century by the Reeves family. Joseph Reeves was a coal merchant and fly proprietor. He kept his horse and small hackney carriage on the premises and plied for trade at Virginia Water station. Walter Reeves continued the coal business, keeping the coal in the small thatched shed just visible in the distant left in the photograph below. Walnut Tree Cottage was demolished in about 1960 and two bungalows built on the site.

STROUDE VILLAGE *c.1908*

By the late 19th century cottagers were expectant of higher standards of housing and between 1880 and 1910 more than 25 villas were built in Stroude, most of them semi-detached and most of them proudly bearing their date and name. *Hope Cottage,* built in 1883, became one of the hamlet's grocer's shops. In 1901 it was also Stroude's post office, kept by William Bowden. Later Elizabeth Bowden took over and she in turn handed over the business to her daughter, May H. West. In the photograph the water tower of Thomas Holloway's sanatorium for the mentally ill, opened in 1885, dominates the skyline. In the early 20th century as cottages in St Ann's Heath and Stroude came on the market they were bought up by Holloway Sanatorium Trustees as further accommodation for staff; *Amelia Cottage* in 1901; *Stroude Villas, Burrell, Ackender* and *Grape Cottages* for £275 each between 1914-18; *Jubilee Cottages* in 1924 for £1,500. The cottages on the left survive and the Royal Standard can be seen in the centre. The road was then still unmetalled and there was no pavement.

DORMAN'S SHOP *Stroude c.1904*

This shop was, until 1989, Stroude's bakers, the bakery chimney visible in the background. George Dorman, as well as selling bread and grocery was an agent for Clarke's, the Egham clock and watch makers.
Mr Dorman took over the Stroude shop on 1 January 1904 and stayed for four years. His mother is standing in the doorway. The Godfrey family ran the business from about 1910, baking bread on the premises and making excellent wedding cakes. In the 1930s the character of the village changed. Building plots along the Stroude Road were carved out of the fields once owned by the Bosher family, corn merchants of Egham. Bungalows, semi-detached and detached houses marched along the fields towards Egham. Luddington Avenue was built. By the late 1930s Stroude houses had numbers as well as names.

SANATORIUM HILL *Stroude Road c.1910*

By 1910 large numbers of the inhabitants of Stroude and St Ann's Heath were involved in the running of the sanatorium; whole families worked there, sons and daughters often following parents in nursing or auxiliary service. Many feet pounded the hill between the sanatorium and Stroude. In June 1954, however, the road was blocked. Tons of earth, stones and uprooted trees had fallen away from sanatorium land after a severe storm. One of the buildings found itself on the edge of a precipice. The land-slide was subsequently made good, the cliff shored up and a substantial wall built to prevent such an event happening again. On the left is one of the sanatorium lodges and halfway down the hill on the right is the house where the sanatorium coachman lived.

HOLLOWAY SANATORIUM *Stroude Road c.1905*

In the mid 19th century there was a fear that insanity was on the increase and Thomas Holloway, who had amassed a fortune from the manufacturing of pills and ointments, was looking for a way of spending some of it. Anything tackled by Mr Holloway was done thoroughly. He attended meetings on mental health, consulted experts and decided that his hospital was to be for the middle classes, 'the professional breadwinner whose income ceases absolutely when he is unable to work'. The site at St Ann's Heath on the Trotsworth estate was chosen and Thomas's wife, Jane, laid the first brick in 1873. The architect was William H. Crossland, who modelled the sanatorium tower on the Cloth Hall at Ypres in Belgium; Holloway himself bought the bricks. The total cost was £219,390. The sanatorium was opened in 1885 by the then Prince and Princess of Wales, later King Edward VII and Queen Alexandra.

HOLLOWAY SANATORIUM *recreation hall c.1905*

The great recreation hall with its magnificant hammer beam roof was Crossland's masterpiece. The general design was based on La Sainte Chapelle in Paris. Around the walls can be seen decorative panels including portraits of national heroes such as Raleigh, Marlborough and Nelson. These cost £25 each. The Royal Family was also depicted, the portrait of Queen Victoria being the most expensive at £38.10s. The portraits of Thomas and Jane Holloway cost £30 each. These and the decorative and floral motifs surrounding them were executed by various artists including students from the Kensington School of Art. It is hoped that these will be restored in the 1989 plans for the transformation of the sanatorium into residential accommodation.

THOMAS HOLLOWAY *1800-1883*

The great entrepreneur is seen here in contemplative mood, probably at his mansion, Tittenhurst Park in Sunninghill. He was the epitome of the self-made man. He was born in Devonport where his parents were grocers and innkeepers. He received enough education to take himself to France at the age of 28. On his return to England he acted as a foreign and commercial agent and became involved with a patent medicine manufacturer. Soon he was making his own products in his mother's pots and pans. After his marriage he worked with his wife, Jane, from four in the morning until ten at night at his works in the Strand, London. He advertised flamboyantly, travelled widely and was involved in the smallest details of his projects until prevented by illness. He died on Boxing Day 1883 and was buried in Sunninghill churchyard, eighteen months before the sanatorium was opened.

HOLLOWAY SANATORIUM
band promenade c.1905

The sanatorium was run on the lines of an English country house at the turn of the century, elegant furniture in rooms and corridors, the grounds laid out for strolling, or playing tennis and cricket. In the photograph a band is performing for the entertainment of staff, patients and visitors.

HOLLOWAY SANATORIUM *the chapel c.1905*

From the 73 certified patients and several boarders admitted in the sanatorium's first year the number of patients increased steadily. The regime was progressive and the environs attractive, and the staff numbers increased with the patients. In the photograph the nurses' choir is seen leaving the chapel after divine service. The building of the chapel cost Holloway £12,500. A small chapel for Roman Catholics was added later. Only one marriage has taken place in the chapel, that of Joy White and Dudley Whitfield in 1957, both bride and groom being nurses at the sanatorium. In the early days of the sanatorium nurses as well as domestic staff lived on the premises. By 1929, however, the number of patients and staff had increased so much that a Nurses' Home was built in Sandy Lane for £22,000. It was opened by Lady Middleton.

HOLLOWAY SANATORIUM *steward's office 1934*

To keep such a large and complex organisation as Holloway Sanatorium running smoothly, managerial as well as medical skills were required. Here the steward, Mr Robertson, is seen in his office with his assistant, Mr Harrison and Mr Philip Bishop. They were responsible for the general management of the house, for the provision of food and for the keeping of household inventories. On 5 July 1948 Holloway Sanatorium ceased to be a private hospital and was absorbed into the National Health Service, becoming administratively part of St Peter's Hospital, Chertsey in 1968.

HOLLOWAY SANATORIUM *the fire 1978*

On 8 February 1978 a disastrous fire broke out on the stage of the cinema, shortly before the showing of *Return of the Daleks.* The fire spread rapidly fanned by a strong easterly wind. The cinema and three wards, 'Clouston', 'Jane Holloway' and 'Thomas Holloway' were completely gutted and the electro-convulsive therapy department and sewing rooms were badly damaged. The patients were calmly escorted from the building by staff and there was only one injury – a patient who fell and grazed his leg. A fire also occurred in 1903 when lightning set fire to the roof causing £1,500 worth of damage. In 1981 the sanatorium closed, its remaining patients being moved to a new wing at St Peter's Hospital, Chertsey.

ST ANN'S HEATH SCHOOL

junction of Trumps Green Road and Sandhills Lane 1974

The population of Virginia Water had more than doubled between 1867 and the late 1890s. The railway and the construction of Holloway Sanatorium had brought much needed work to the district. More families came in, more cottages were built, the birth rate was rising and Christ Church, the village's only school, was crowded. The Egham School Board, therefore, decided to build a new school, a 'board' or state school at St Ann's Heath. It opened on 20 October 1896 with 111 pupils on the register, 57 in the Mixed School and 54 in the Infant Department. Only two staff were initially appointed to instruct these children: the headmistress, Miss E. Atkin, assisted by Miss G. Hunt who had only just completed her pupil-teacher training. Thirty-seven children from Christ Church School transferred to St Ann's and their teachers attended the opening ceremony. The building continued to serve the local community until 1975 when a new school was opened in Sandhills Lane. The old building was eventually demolished and a block of flats built on the school site.

ST ANN'S HEATH SCHOOL *classroom c.1929*

This photograph will take many readers back to their childhood days: to the smell of polish and disinfectant, to the little flat desks with holes for the inkwells and the picture of the Good Shepherd on the wall. The two classrooms shown had originally been one large room. The half-glass partition enabled two classes to be taught more conveniently. The headmaster, Mr Harwood taught the top class in the far room and was able to keep an eye on the younger children and their teacher through the glass. A class photograph was obviously a serious matter. One can almost hear the command: 'Sit up straight and put your hands behind your back'.

ST ANN'S HEATH SCHOOLBOYS

visiting Brooklands 1933

The afternoon of Empire Day was always a holiday and thus it was that several boys were taken to Brooklands on 24 May 1933. There they experienced the thrill of a flight in a German Junkers type F.13ge, a single engined, five passenger, low wing cabin monoplane, designed in 1919. This particular model had been imported into England in 1930 and only acquired by Brooklands Airways Ltd in April 1933. The pilot, on the lower left in the photograph, is thought to be Captain Fielden. Two of the boys, Reg Cox on the extreme left and Tim Hayes, second from the right, became Virginia Water postmen. The other adult in the picture is George Broomfield, Virginia Water station's booking clerk in the 1930s and 40s. In the early years of the century he became involved in the flying machine experiments of Samuel Cody and in 1911 made the world's first 'wing-walk'. He afterwards saw active service repairing aircraft with the Royal Flying Corps in France in the First World War.

MEADOWSWEET SPORTS

The Paddock, Stroude Road c.1952

The photograph shows Carol Othen competing in the Meadowsweet Sports, a tradition that began 32 years earlier. In 1918 Charles Oscar Gridley, of *Meadowsweet* in Stroude, created the Meadowsweet Memorial Trust in memory of 'my dear wife and all her gentle ways'. The dividends from his investment were 'to give pleasure and recreation' to the children of Virginia Water. Mr Gridley suggested that an annual sports day should be held, that there should be prizes given for a knowledge of wild flowers and that teas should be provided for competitors and officials. From 1920 onwards the wild flower competition was held at Christ Church and St Ann's Heath Schools, sometimes judged in the early days by Mr Gridley himself. On the Friday nearest 22 July each year the two schools met on the sports field, Holloway Sanatorium's Paddock in Stroude Road. Even during the rationing of the Second World War teas were provided by the parents and helpers for nearly 400 people, no mean feat 'in such difficult times'. By the 1960s, however, though the Meadowsweet Sports were still held, the numbers were too great for the schools to combine.

DUMMY BOMB *at the Clockcase 1914-1918*

In the First World War Canadian troops set up a lumber camp in Windsor Great Park. One of their duties was felling trees in the Clockcase Plantation where the dummy bomb was found. During their stay in the park, the Canadians were reviewed by King George V and Queen Mary. When children were sent out to collect the wood chippings at the lumber sites the soldiers often helped the little ones to fill their baskets with wood.

THE VIRGINIA WATER FOOTBALL CLUB *1920-21*

In 1919 a group of young Virginia Water men formed a football team and played friendly matches locally. Most of them were born in Thorpe or Virginia Water, two worked locally and six of them had served with the 6th East Surrey Regiment in India, during the First World War. The following year Alfred Bishop, second from the left in the back row, founded the club and entered it into league football by joining the North West Surrey Minor League. They did so well they were runners-up in their first season. This photograph celebrated the event. They played at the Paddock in Stroude Road by courtesy of the Holloway Sanatorium authorities and later adopted the red and green colours of the sanatorium. In the 1930s the club received the patronage of Edward, Prince of Wales, later King Edward VIII, then living at Fort Belvedere. The patronage was continued by HM King George VI and by HM Queen Elizabeth II. In 1972 a new clubhouse was opened in Crown Road by Sir Stanley Rous, one time president of FIFA. The clubhouse was named *The Timbers* in honour of Harry Timbers who served the club as secretary for more than 35 years. By then the club had graduated through several football leagues to the Combined Counties League.

THE STAG AND HOUNDS *Wellington Avenue 1925*

After the demolition of the old hostelry in 1922 Robert Hammond retained the licence by serving beer from a tin shed which still survives at the rear of the new pub. His family moved to Longcross until the new building opened. Robert and his wife, Amy, are seen here next to the Crossley open tourer which had probably come down from London. The beer did not have to come far, only from Ashby's brewery in Staines. Later the Reading brewery Simonds took over. Today the Stag, as it is called locally, is a Courage house. Originally there were three bars with a central door into the largest. In the 1960s the internal walls were removed, making one large bar and the central entrance was blocked in. A small piece of the old 19th century beerhouse — the wall behind the bar — was retained in the new structure.

STATION GREEN *now Station Approach c.1939*

Included in Tarrant's plan for the Wentworth Estate was this parade of shops tastefully built in mock-Tudor, today recognised by architectural historians as a specific style. This picture shows the first stage, the flats above the shops and between the gable ends having wooden balconies constructed by skilled joiners using pegged joints. The parade was incomplete at the outbreak of war in 1939. The gaps were filled in in the 1950s but the fine woodwork and balconies were omitted in the postwar work.

WENTWORTH AT WAR *1939-45*

With the commencement of hostilities in 1939 many service and other departments were moved out of London. The close proximity of a number of sizeable properties to one another made Wentworth, Shrubbs Hill and Broomhall natural venues and a number of properties were requisitioned. Extensive installations were built under Wentworth House. The Dormy House, previously Portnall, became an officers' club and its excellent dances, in what had been the De Salis family ballroom, were popular locally. Enemy action in February 1944 resulted in the death of two residents at *Warrenbayne* in West Drive. Virginia Water had its own Home Guard detachment. Here can be seen Private J. Mitchell of Trumps Green and Corporal Hayward of Knowle Hill talking to HM King George VI at *Bears House* in Portnall Rise.

VICTORY CELEBRATIONS AT TRUMPS GREEN *1945*

The little community at Trumps Green celebrated victory in a big way with a street party at the east end of Trumps Green Avenue. Here the Army Cadets' band is approaching from Trumps Green Road. Tortosa Cottages can be seen in the left background and Wellesley Cottages on the right. The grass patch on the right is now occupied by Pitch and Chip – Don Couzens' fish and chip shop. Leading the band is Frank Ponsford. From the victory party came the idea of a Community Association and a small group of local residents met in December 1946 to discuss the project. A ways and means committee was elected to investigate the building of a community centre. By January 1949 £587 had been raised by bazaars, dances etc. Building on a site in Cabrera Avenue commenced in June 1949 and while work on the main shell was carried out by professionals most of the internal work was done by members. The hall was officially opened on 1 April 1950. It is still very much used with a number of weekly activities and an annual horticultural, craft and cookery show.

THE PARTY SITE IN TRUMPS GREEN AVENUE *1945*

Although the road now has a better surface and some of the telegraph poles have gone, little has changed. The fashions and the size of the prams define the date. Locals call this end of Trumps Green Avenue 'The White City' as many of the houses are painted white.

FANCY DRESS PARADE *1945*

Even after years of austerity mums were still able to find a little finery for the fancy dress parades. The European allies were represented by the 'little Dutch boy' in the centre. Christopher Morris came as the bridegroom with a young Miss Tester as his bride. In the background left, with open neck shirt, is Mr Oliver, Trumps Green's resident policeman at the time. By the telegraph pole is the then headmaster of St Ann's Heath School, Mr S. E. Clout.

TARRANT BUILDERS LTD *'The Evesham' c.1956*

Following the failure of Tarrant's company in 1931, the business re-emerged as Tarrant Builders Ltd but without him in command. The firm continued to build large high quality houses up to the Second World War. However in the early 1940s the company was taken over by Sir Lindsay Parkinson & Co Ltd. To a lesser extent the production of large houses continued but the company decided in the 1950s to proceed with the production of a number of designs of speculation built houses in the Trumps Green and Knowle Hill areas. *The Evesham* was built in Cabrera and Harpesford Avenues and advertised as 'a semi-detached house to please the discerning purchaser'. They cost £2,450, a deposit of £275 being required.

TARRANT BUILDERS LTD *'The Clifton' 1959*

The Clifton was built in Harpesford Avenue, Crown Road and Wellington Avenue. A trio is seen here, the last sod of the quarter acre gardens just dug. Hot water was supplied by a back-boiler in the living room. Until the harsh winter of 1962-63 speculation builders and purchasers alike seemed indifferent to such creature comforts as central heating. *The Clifton* design lent itself well to being extended and few houses remain as first built. They were sold in 1959 for just £3,350. Tarrant Builders had no trouble in selling. The market had been well researched.

VIRGINIA WATER METHODIST CHURCH

Cabrera Avenue 1959

In April 1947 Mr A. D. Budd, a well known lay-reader who lived in Lennox Cottage, Wellington Avenue, got together a small group of local Methodists. They afterwards started to meet for evening worship in Trotsworth Hall, Virginia Water. Later, services were transferred to the Trumps Green Community Centre in Cabrera Avenue. From these beginnings, plans were made to purchase land, and these were realised when a site was found, next to the Community Centre. It was backed by woodland which sloped down to the River Bourne. Under the leadership of the Superintendent Minister, the Reverend G. W. Underwood, the architects, Highet & Phillips of Guildford, and the builder, E. P. Wickens & Sons of Chertsey, were chosen. The local Methodist Society applied itself conscientiously to raise contributions towards the cost. The stone laying ceremony was conducted in November 1958 in the presence of many of the churches in the Staines and Feltham Circuit, as well as churchmen of other denominations, including the Reverend R. H. Walker of Christ Church, Virginia Water. The church was opened on 27 June 1959 by Miss Doris Smith, Secretary to the Women's Meeting and one of the original group who had met in 1947, and whose ambitions were finally realised.

Photographer: Kenneth W. Fensom

VIRGINIA WATER METHODIST CHURCH

view of the sanctuary 1959

The communion table with its two silver flower vases and the font with its brass interior were made by Roger Wood and Michael Williamson, students at the former Shoreditch Teacher Training College at Englefield Green. The work was done as part of their examination projects. Oak for the communion table and the font was paid for by the Women's Fellowship members and Miss Doris Smith respectively. A plaque on the vestibule wall records the church's gratitude to The Joseph Rank Benevolent Trust, The London Mission and the Chapel Committee. A generous grant from the Trustees of the Waterloo Road Methodist Church enabled the work and witness of this bombed out London church to continue in Virginia Water.

Photographer: Kenneth W. Fensom

TRUMPS GREEN ROAD *1987*

Many people were woken in the early hours of Friday 16 October 1987 by the noise of crashing timber and even breaking glass. Others, mostly snug behind double glazing, slept peacefully on while the worst storm in living memory caused havoc in the south of England. They woke to find no trains moving and many roads blocked. A giant tree had crashed across the A30 near Royal Holloway and Bedford New College and in Wellington Avenue several trees were down. Trumps Green Road, near the railway bridge, was blocked. Council staff soon appeared and local inhabitants, unable to get to work, came out with power and hand saws to clear the debris; others helped to divert traffic. For Wentworth Golf Club in the midst of the Suntory World Match Play Tournament the devastation was appalling. Fortunately a forestry team was at hand working on the new South Course. They combined their efforts with the Estate staff, tournament organisers and volunteers. With a few modifications the tournament continued. By the following afternoon the Estate roads were passable. In history, however, very little is new. In 1866 the Reverend F. J. Rawlins in his *Notes on Virginia Water* reported that a great storm in January that year had not only sunk ships in the Bay of Biscay, but had felled or damaged 6,000 trees in Windsor Great Park, including one of the oldest beech trees in the forest.